100 Easy Smoothie Recipes for Kids

Bonus Green Smoothies for Kids

by Debbie Madson, Madson Web Publishing, LLC

www.kids-cooking-activities.com

contrary interpretation of the subject matter herein. This book is presented solely for motivational and informational purposes only.

Smoothie Recipes for Kids-Why they're great!

Smoothies are an ideal snack for growing kids. In our world of quick, unhealthy snack solutions, it can be hard to make sure your children are getting all the nutrients they need. Add to this the fact that kids are often put off vegetables and fruit because these foods don't have the advertising dollars behind them as certain brands of hamburgers and sugar-loaded cereals. So, it can be hard to even persuade your kids to polish off the vegetables on their plate or eat the apple you put in their lunch box.

Smoothies eliminate some of these problems because you don't have to convince the kids to eat anything. If a smoothie tastes good with oranges or strawberries, you can add a stick of celery or two and half the time kids won't even notice the difference. It's a good way to sneak a few extra nutrients into their diet "under the radar."

But ultimately, you want your kids to be in on what goes in their smoothies and start making their own. In this way smoothies can become a great nutritional teaching tool as kids learn that healthy snacks can also taste great.

How to Get Your Kids Involved

Kids are always more likely to eat something healthy if they have a hand in preparing it, and that preparation is fun. So, one of the keys to getting kids interested in making smoothies is making the whole process exciting and fun.

One important tip is to keep the recipes simple at first. The easier a smoothie is to make, the faster a kid can pick up the process– and often just being able to do it will inspire your child's enthusiasm. Obviously the younger the child the more help and supervision they will need, but you can let them do things like putting the fruit in the blender and pushing the blend button.

Also, don't be too restrictive on the ingredients you allow in smoothies for kids. You should try to make them healthy, but there's nothing wrong with a dollop of ice cream or some chocolate sprinkles here and there. Just make sure the smoothies lean more towards the healthy ingredients, rather than becoming just another fatty, sugary snack.

When it comes time to make a smoothie, make sure you talk it up. Be excited about it yourself and your kids will follow suit. Try to use different variations when it comes to recipes and be prepared to experiment with some out-of-the-box food combinations. Of course, with that in mind, you can always bribe a reluctant kid by adding a bit of their favorite food – a dollop of peanut butter can be a great secret weapon.

Great ideas for Simple Smoothie Recipes

Add cream of coconut to a recipe.

Experiment with different juices including vegetable juices.

Try adding a handful of carrots or celery to the smoothie recipe. Once it is blended nobody will know it is an extra healthy smoothie.

Add up to 1 tablespoon sugar or honey for a sweeter flavor.

Add oat bran, almonds, or wheat germ for an extra burst of nutrition.

If using canned fruit include the juice for extra flavor.

Add 1 tablespoon peanut butter to your smoothie recipe.

Substitute milk for juice or juice for the milk in any recipe.

To make any simple smoothie recipe thinner add more juice or milk. To make any simple smoothie recipe thicker add more fruit.

Simple Smoothie Tips

I wanted to comment on smoothies. They are so nutritious and fun to make. In a blender, I use oranges, apples, pineapple, bananas and blueberries or strawberries and blend them together.

One additional suggestion: Throw in some carrots, or celery or some other veggies and blend in with the fruits. It doesn't change the taste, just the color and children get their fruits and vegetables all at once. St. Patrick's Day is ideal for green smoothies. Just add celery, spinach, or cabbage.

Smoothies are also great for kids to make if they are younger, they can easily add the ingredients to the blender and turn on the button with an adult supervising.

Contents

Strawberry Smoothies

Really Simple Strawberry and Banana Smoothie

One chopped ripe banana
Strawberry yogurt (the regular little cups bought in the stores)
Blend until the right thickness.
One banana and one strawberry yogurt equals a half a cup (or a regular kids cup.)

Strawberry Ice Smoothie

by Cydney (IL)
1 cup strawberries
1 cup low fat milk
1/2 cup vanilla yogurt
1 cup ice
Blend all in blender on high or until smooth.

Easy & Tasty Strawberry

1 banana
1/2 cup strawberries
3/4 cup milk
2 tablespoon sugar
8 ice cubes
Blend all in blender until ice cubes are smooth.

Layered Strawberry Banana Smoothie

by Haleh
1 apple
1 banana
1/2 Cup strawberries
1 Cup milk
4 tablespoons plain yogurt
Instructions:
Put all the ingredients in the blender and blend it all together for about 1 minute, pour it in a glass and decorate it if you want.
Decorating materials:
1 strawberry
gummy bears (optional)
chocolate chips
whipped cream (chocolate or vanilla)
Decorating instructions:
Pour half of the smoothie in your glass, put a layer of whipped cream, chocolate chips and gummy bears and pour the rest of the smoothie on top! then cut the strawberry in tiny pieces and put it on top followed by another layer of whipped cream!

Cucumber Strawberry

1 cucumber, peeled and sliced
5-6 strawberries
Blend all together.

Strawberry Banana Twist

by Andrea (United States)
1/2 Banana
1 cup strawberries
Flax seed (optional)
1 cup plain/vanilla yogurt
4 ice cubes
1/4-1/2 can frozen fruit juice (optional)
2 T. water
Cut up all fruits and put all ingredients in blender. Blend until smooth.
Serves 2-3

Strawberry Sensation

by Andrea (Canada)
Handful of Strawberries (frozen or fresh)
A scoop of Frozen fat free yogurt
2 splashes of guava juice
3 ice cubes
Blend until all ingredients are mixed.

Mummy's Berry and Banana whirl

by Emily (England)
1/2 Cup of fresh strawberries
1/2 Cup of fresh raspberries

1/2 a banana
a teaspoon of apple juice
Put all ingredients in blender and blend until smooth. Fill 2/3 of a glass with ice and pour the smoothie into the glass. Serve with a straw and a slice of strawberry.

Orange Smoothies

Strawberry Orange

1 cup of strawberries (frozen is best)
1 cup of crushed ice
1 cup of orange juice or 2 oranges peeled and sectioned
2 containers of any yogurt
Mix in blender until smooth!

Sunrise Smoothie

by Leigh Ann
1/2 Cup orange juice Fruity Sunrise
1/2 Cup peach juice
2 Tablespoons Maraschino cherry juice
5 Maraschino cherries
Mix orange juice and peach juice. Top with cherry juice, allowing it to blend in slowly making it look like a sunrise. Drop in Maraschino cherries and serve.

Ornanaberry

by Ciara (Las Vegas)
1 Cup of orange juice
1 Cup strawberry yogurt (or other type of fruit yogurt)
1 banana (diced or sliced)
1/4 Cup of blueberries
4 ice cubes
1/2 Cup of milk
1 teaspoon of vanilla
Blend together.

Orange Sunrise Smoothie

by Ashley (California)
1 can of pineapple slices
1 cup of orange juice
1 whole banana
1/2 cup of %2 low-fat milk
1 cup of ice
Put the pineapple slices, orange juice, banana, and milk all together into the blender. Mix them up and one at a time add the ice cubes through the blender tube.

Orange Julius

6oz. orange juice concentrate
2 cups milk
1/4 Cup sugar
2 teaspoons vanilla
5 ice cubes
Blend together until ice is crushed.

Apple Orange Banana Smoothie

by Jennifer (Utah)
1 Apple peeled and cut into slices
1 Orange peeled with pulp off and sectioned
1 Banana peeled and cut into slices
Ice cubes (as many as it takes or as many as you want)
1 Cup of orange juice
Now what you want to do is add everything together into the blender. Then you want to mix it all. Make sure that you mix it until it is how you want it or until it is smooth. Then you can do what I like to do and put it in a fancy cup with a drink umbrella and treat your children like royalty. I know that my children love it and they tell me that it feels like they're in Hawaii. Enjoy!

Citrus Smoothie

2 T. lime juice
1 orange (or tangerine) peeled
2 T. lemon juice

2 Cups orange juice
8 oz. yogurt any flavor or plain
Feel free to add any strawberries, bananas, apples, or any other fruit for flavor
Blend until smooth.

Banana Smoothies

Banana Buzz Smoothie

by Branko (Australia)
2 halved bananas
1 teaspoon of honey (optional)
5-8 blocks of ice
1/2 cup of milk
Blend until smooth.

Strawberry Banana Protein Smoothie

1-2 Bananas
4 strawberries
1 small container of vanilla yogurt
1 Big Cup of Ice
A Little Dash of Protein Powder
Blend until smooth.

The Berry-Bonanza Smoothie

1 cup of milk
2 cups frozen fruit
1 sliced banana
1 Cup vanilla yogurt
Blend until smooth.

Banana Heaven

by Kimberley (England)
3 bananas chopped
1-2 Cups of milk
1 Cup of yogurt any flavor
1/2 cup of ice cubes
Blend all together.

Banana Smoothie

by Hallie (OH)
1 banana chopped
1/2 cup V-8 fruit juice any flavor
Blend together.

Easy Banana Squeeze

by Chloe (Newcastle)
2 Bananas
3 scoops of banana/vanilla ice cream or yogurt
1 Cup of milk.
Blend for 1 minute for perfect results and serve in glass with real dairy cream squirted on in a spiral, it is a good idea to add a slice of banana on top. For my kids as a little treat, I often sprinkle hundreds and thousands/ sprinkles on top.

Banana Protein

by Nicole (MN)
1 banana (cut up)
2 Tablespoons sugar
1/2 Cup milk
1 oz. protein powder
Mix in blender.

New York Style Banana Smoothie

1-5 bananas
3 tablespoons of orange juice
1/2 Cup ice cubes
1 Cup yogurt
Mix ingredients together in a blender and blend until completely smooth

Mostly, Banana Smoothie

3-5 Bananas
1/2 T. of Honey
1/2 Cup of almond (to make it crunchy),
1 Cup of milk,
3-4 ice cubes
Blend until smooth.

Banana Peach smoothie

by Garett & Shelby (N.M)
First, you will need a banana, milk, and a peach yogurt. Cut up the banana and put it in the blender along with peach yogurt and 1 cup of milk then blend it until creamy.

Mixed Fruits Smoothie

The Fruity Samba!

by Chrystyna (Canada)
12 Strawberries
1 Nectarine or peach
1/4 Cup plain yogurt
1/4 Cup or less sugar
A splash of lemon juice (optional)
Blend and enjoy!!

Berry Banana Pineapple

1 medium banana
a handful blueberries
5 pineapple slices
2-5 ice cubes
Blend until smooth.

Fruitie Tootie Smoothie!

by Danii
1 Banana peeled
1 orange peeled
6 frozen strawberries
1 1/2 cups of orange juice
Blend until smooth.

Fruit Salad Smoothie

by Sarah
1 small tin fruit salad (and juice too)
1 small tub yogurt
hand full of ice cubes
Just put it all and the blender and enjoy.
Place a dollop of whip cream on top of every individual smoothie!

The Smoothie Mix

Pour a little bit of orange juice and milk in a blender.
Next throw in some strawberries or other frozen fruit. Then any type of yogurt, I put in blueberry yogurt. Then put some ice cubes in for thickness.

Carrot Smoothie

Yummy fruit smoothie with a secret

by Matilda (South Africa)
This is very nice, and my kids absolutely love this!
1 banana, cut in pieces
4-5 strawberries
handful of grapes
1 pear sliced
1/2 Cup Mango juice or other tropical flavor
3-4 slices of Pineapple
2 Carrots, cut in chunks (secret ingredient)
5-6 ice cubes
Start with the juice and carrots and make sure the carrots are blended very finely. Thereafter you can add the other fruit and the ice. This is absolutely delicious.

Mango Smoothies

Mango and Strawberries Smoothie

by Ashleigh (Australia)
1 Cup of mango slices
4 large strawberries
1 scoop of strawberry yogurt
1 Cup of orange juice
10 ice cubes
Put into a blender and blend until smooth

Mango Smoothie

2 1/2 cups of Mango Juice
1 Cup of Vanilla yogurt or plain
1 Sliced Banana
Blend all ingredients together.

Mango, Coconut, and Passion Fruit Shake

by Alice (Georgia)
1 large mango peeled, or 1 1/4 cups of mango puree
6 large passion fruit, or 2/3 cup of passion fruit juice
3/4 cup of coconut milk
12 ice cubes
Instructions:
Cut the mango flesh away from the pit. Coarsely chop the flesh and put into a blender. Cut the passion fruit in half and scoop the seeds into a strainer set over a bowl. Use a spoon to press down the seeds and extract all the juice. Add the juice, coconut milk, and ice cubes to the blender and puree until smooth.

Mango Tropical

by Jessica (CA)
2 sliced and peeled bananas
1 half can of dole pineapple
1 1/2 Cups of strawberry
1-2 bananas
half a mango
1-2 scoops coconut ice cream or yogurt
Blend until smooth

Mawi Delisiouso

by Alexa (Michigan)
2 kiwis, peeled and cut in half
1 mango, peeled and cut in pieces
1 1/2 Cup of orange juice
1 Cup of ice or more if you want
First put in the mango and kiwis and orange juice. When all of that is blended, put in the ice. Blend until smooth

Mango Smoothie

3 scoops of mango sorbet
1 Cup of mango yogurt
1/2 Cup milk
1 Cup crushed ice cubes
1 banana (sliced)
Mix in a blender until smooth.

Mango Banana Coconut

by Hannah (OR)
2 soft mangoes, peeled and cut in pieces
1 Cup of milk
2 bananas, cut in slices
1/2 Cup of strawberries
1/4 Cup coconut (optional)
Add to blender and mix till smooth

Watermelon Smoothies

Summer Smoothie

by Matilda (South Africa)
1 mango, peeled and cut in pieces
2 Cups watermelon cut in pieces
1 orange peeled and sectioned
1 carrot, peeled and cut in slices
4-5 ice cubes
Blend all together and enjoy.

Watermelon Smoothie

by Shanna and Kaitlynn (WI)
6 or so pieces, cut up cantaloupe
10 or so frozen strawberries
2 pinches of sugar
4 medium sized watermelon chunks
1/2 Cup of regular pineapple juice
1/2 Cup of vanilla yogurt
Blend until smooth.

Peach Smoothies

Peach Banana Fizz Smoothie

by Julie and Phil
1 Nectarine or peach, cut in slices
1 Peach flavored yogurt
1 Plum, cut in half
2 tablespoons of Sugar (optional)
1 teaspoon of Cinnamon
1 3/4 cups of Milk
5 Ice cubes
2 Bananas
Blend together until smooth!

Strawberry Peach Swizzle

by Katie (Ireland)
1 Cup of strawberries
1/2 Cup of yogurt, any flavor or plain
1/2 Cup of chopped banana
1 sliced peach
1 Cup of ice cubes
1 Cup of orange juice
1/2 Cup of strawberry juice
Blend all together.

Peach Banana Berry

by Savanna (USA)
5 strawberries
4 peaches, cut in slices
2 bananas, cut in slices
2 Tbsp. of honey
1 1/4 Cup milk
6 ice cubes
Blend all together.

Fruit Smoothie

by Taylor (MO)
2 Cups of peach slices
1 Cup of apricot slices
1 Cup of fruit cocktail
1/2 Cup of milk
4-5 ice cubes
Blend in blender until liquid and no more ice chunks.

Blueberry Smoothies

Blueberry Strawberry

1/2 Cup ice cubes
1/2 Cup orange juice
1/2 Cup strawberries
1/2 Cup blueberries
Add all ingredients to blender and blend until ice cubes are crushed.

Rainbow Smoothie

by Ashley (Georgia)
1/2 Cup orange juice
1 Cup mixed raspberries or berry mixture
1/2 Cup milk
1/2 Cup crushed ice
1 Cup yogurt
1 banana
Blend together.

Sherbet Berry

by Abby (Wisconsin)
1 1/2 Cups Blueberries
As much as you need/want of Orange Sherbet
1/4 cup or less milk
Blend well.

Super Berry Smoothie

by Jessy (VA)
1 Cup blueberries
1/2 Cup blackberries
1/2 Cup raspberries
1/2 Cup white grape juice
1 Cup strawberry yogurt
1/2 Cup ice cubes (optional)
Add all ingredients together in a blender and blend together until smooth.

Fruit Craze Smoothie

by Blair (USA)
1 Cup frozen strawberries
1/2 Cup fresh or frozen raspberries, blueberries, banana pieces
1/2 Cup milk
2 tbsp. sugar
Add ingredients together into the blender and blend until smooth.

Strawberry & Blueberry Deluxe Smoothie

Add about a cup of ice
1 1/2 Cups Milk
1/2 Cup blueberries
3 Strawberries
1 1/2 T. Sugar
Add all ingredients to blender and blend until ice cubes are crushed.

Purple Tummy Yummy

by Breanna (OK)
2 frozen bananas, skins removed and cut in chunks
1/2 Cup frozen blueberries
1 Cup orange juice
1 teaspoon honey(optional)
1 teaspoon vanilla extract (optional)
Add all ingredients to blender and blend until smooth.

Apple Smoothies

Apple and Ice

1 apple, sliced
1 cup of ice
a splash of apple juice
Add all ingredients to blender and blend until ice cubes are crushed.

Apple Orange Smoothie

by Ryan
2 oranges, peeled and sectioned
1 apple, peeled and cut in slices
1/2 Cup orange juice
5 ice cubes
Add all ingredients to blender and blend until smooth.

Simple Banana and Apple Blast

1 apple, cored and sliced
1 banana, sliced
1 Cup natural yogurt
1/4 Cup milk
pinch of sugar
Add ingredients together in a blender and blend until smooth.

Healthy Fruit Smoothie Blend

by Jacque (California)
1/3 cup pineapple (plus juice)
1 cored and sliced apple
1 peeled frozen banana
5 fresh strawberries
1/2 Cup vanilla yogurt
1 scoop of any flavor protein powder
Blend until smooth.

Grape Smoothie

Grape and Strawberry

2 apples peeled and cut in slices
6 strawberries
a handful of grapes
1/2 cup ice cubes
Add all together and blend until smooth.

Grape Orange

1 Cup grapes
1 orange peeled and sliced
1 Cup frozen fruit
Blend until nice and smooth.

Coconut Smoothies

Jungle Smoothie

by Clarissa (North Carolina)
1 Cup coconut milk
1 half banana
1/2 Cup orange juice
1/4 Cup assorted berries
2 scoops vanilla yogurt or ice cream
Put milk and ice cream in blender for 1 minute. Add banana, orange juice, and berries. Blend for 3 minutes.

Coconut Smoothie

by Sarah (England)
1/2 Cup coconut
1 Cup coconut milk
2 T. vanilla yogurt
1/2 Cup of crushed ice
Add all ingredients to blender and blend until ice cubes are crushed.

Hawaii Coconut and Mango Smoothie

by Jayden (WI)
2 soft mangoes, peeled cut in pieces
2 soft coconuts peeled
1/2 Cup milk
4 ice cubes
Add all ingredients to blender and blend until ice cubes are crushed.

Pincocoaya

by Cassie (Nanaimo)
2-3 pineapple slices
1 Cup coconut milk
1 papaya, cut in pieces
1 banana sliced
2 Cups of ice
1/2 Cup water
Blend together until desired thickness

Raspberry Smoothie

Banana Berry

1 banana, cut in slices
1 Cup milk
2 ice cubes
2 Cups frozen raspberries
Mix in blender until ice is crushed.

Super Berry Smoothie

2 Cups raspberries (fresh or frozen)
1/2 Cup milk
1 Cup orange juice
4 ice cubes
Blend thoroughly until smooth.

Mixed Berry

2 Cups frozen mixed berries
1 tsp of sugar
1 1/2 Cups milk
1 1/2 Cups yogurt (any flavor)
Put the mixed berries, milk, and yogurt in the blender. Blend it together.
When it is smooth add the sugar, then blend it for another 15 seconds.

Banana Berry

2 Cups of orange juice
2 bananas
2 handfuls of raspberries
Blend together until smooth.

Very Berry

2 Cups raspberries or berries
1 Cup vanilla yogurt
2 teaspoons of sugar
1/2 Cup of ice (crushed or cubed)
Mix ingredients in a blender until smooth.

Kiwi Smoothies

Raspberry and Kiwi

2-3 Cups of sliced kiwi
2-3 Cups of raspberries
1 Cup of ice
1 Cup of any yogurt
Blend together and enjoy

Kiwi Strawberry Smoothie

by Jessica (CA)
5-8 Strawberries
4 kiwis (peeled and cut in half)
1 cup of milk
1 tablespoon vanilla
1/2 cup ice
Blend until smooth. Serves 2

Strawberry Kiwi

by DeAsarae (Indiana)
1 Cup of frozen strawberries
4 kiwis', cut in pieces
2 Cups of any fruity drink
3/4 Cup of soy milk

Blend.

Fruit Blend Smoothie

1 Cup fresh strawberries
1 banana cut into pieces
2 Cups orange juice
a little over one cup of milk (2%)
1 kiwi skinned and cut into pieces
Blend until smooth.

Pineapple Smoothie

Tutti Frutti Smoothie

1/2 banana
4 strawberries
2 spoonful frozen pineapple concentrate
1 mixed berry yogurt
a hint of vanilla
Blend until smooth.

Strawberry and "Pinana" Swoosh

by Alicia (Wisconsin)
2 Cups strawberries
1 Cup banana
1 can of pineapple with juice
8.5 oz. of yogurt any flavor
Blend everything together except one cup strawberries and 4.25 oz. of yogurt. After all is liquidated put aside. Take your remaining yogurt and strawberries and mix them together separately; mush the strawberries in. Pour in smoothie mixture.

Pineapple Strawberry Banana

by Beth (Northumberland)
1/4 of pineapple juice carton
3 bananas
1 small carton plain yogurt
4-5 strawberries

2 tsp of honey (if needed to sweeten)
Blend together until smooth.

Banana Pineapple

by Brooke Ann (USA)
1 1/2 Cups of pineapple juice
2 Cups of chopped frozen banana
1/2 Cup vanilla yogurt
1/2 T. of honey
Place all ingredients in blender and process until smooth.

Apple Berry Pine Nana

by Kristen (CA)
1 Cup frozen strawberries
1/2 Cup frozen mixed berries
1/2 Cup frozen pineapple pieces
1 sliced and cored apple
1 peeled and sliced banana
1 Cup plain frozen yogurt
1 Cup orange juice
1/2 Cup milk
2 tablespoons sugar
Blend until smooth.

Banana, Coconut, and Pineapple

by Rainey (Ohio)
1-2 bananas, cut in slices
1/2 Cup of creamed coconut
1 Cup of crushed pineapple
3 Cups of ice
Add pineapple, bananas, coconut, then add ice gradually. Blend till smooth.

Hawaiian Smoothie

by Jessica (CA)
1 can of dole pineapple
2 Cups of coconut milk
1 Cup of ice
1 Cup of orange juice
2 scoops of vanilla yogurt
Blend until smooth

Blackberry Smoothie

Berry Dream

by Natasha (Scotland)
2 Cups Strawberries (fresh or frozen)
1 Cup raspberries (fresh or frozen)
1 Cup blackberries (fresh or frozen)
4 or more ice cubes
Put in blender and blend until smooth

Berry Yogurt Smoothie

1 Cup raspberries, blackberries, or strawberries
2 Tablespoons of vanilla yogurt
1 Cup orange juice
1 Cup milk
Put in blender and blend until smooth

Moolicious Berry Smoothie

by Mallika (Pennsylvania)
8-10 blackberries
1 banana, peeled and sliced
1 Cup 2% milk
1 teaspoon of sugar
Blend all ingredients together. Pour into glass and enjoy with a purple straw!

Berry Blast

by Sintajah (Atlanta)
1 Cup strawberries, blackberries, or raspberries
4-5 ice cubes
Place berries in blender or food processor with ice and let blend on high or medium.
Let blend until completely processed. Stir and serve.

Yumberry smoothie

1/2 Cup blueberries
1/2 Cup blackberries
1/4 Cup strawberries
1 Cup milk
Blend and enjoy

Dessert Smoothies

Chocolate Smoothie

by Gwen (Illinois)
1/2 Cup chocolate chips
1 whole banana
1/2 Cup strawberries
1/2 Cup milk
Blend together. Put in a glass with whipped cream on top and it is delicious!
If you chose you can top the whip cream with chocolate chips or M&M's.

Strawberry Banana Blitz

by Keira (Canada)
8 sliced strawberries
1 sliced banana
3 scoops of ice cream
1/2 cup milk
10 ice cubes
Add all ingredients to blender. Blend until smooth.

Lemonade smoothie

by Alyssa (buffalo)
2 tablespoons of lemon juice
3 ice cubes
2 teaspoons of sugar
1/2 cup of lemon or lemon meringue pie yogurt

blend for 20 seconds for your awesome lemony smoothie.

Banana Chocolate Smoothie

2 small bananas
2/3 Cup chocolate chips
2/3 Cup milk
1/2 Cup ice-cubes
1/4 Cup yogurt
Blend until smooth.

Jell-O Berry Smoothie

1/2 Cup milk (add more if flavor is too tangy)
1/2 cup strawberries
1/2 Cup ice cubes
1 Cup yogurt
1 Packet of Jell-O (My kids love the mixed berry Jell-O)
Add ingredients in blender and blend until smooth.

Banana Chocolate

4 ice cubes
2 spoons of vanilla yogurt
1 Cup of milk
1 banana

chocolate syrup
Blend until smooth. Drizzle top with chocolate syrup.

Banana Surprise

by Victoria (Canada)
2 Bananas
4 Strawberries
2 regular cups of yogurt, any flavor
2 regular cups of chocolate pudding bought in store.
OR
3 scoops of ice cream. Any flavor.

Banana Nesquick Smoothie

3/4 Cups milk
1/2 Cup ice
1/2 medium banana
1/4 Cup Orange Juice
3 Tbsp. strawberry Nesquick powder mix.
Directions:

Put all ingredients in your blender and blend until smooth. I put more than 1/2 cup of ice to make it thicker. Pour into glasses and top with a scoop of ice cream or whip cream on top.

Pumpkin Milkshake

1/2 Cup pumpkin puree
3/4 Cup vanilla yogurt
1/2 Cup milk
1-2 scoops vanilla ice cream
1/4 teaspoon cinnamon
1/8 teaspoon nutmeg
Add all ingredients to blender. Blend until smooth.

Fruit Galore Smoothie

by Tucker (CA)
3 Scoops Vanilla Ice Cream
2 Scoops Strawberry Ice Cream
1/2 Cup orange juice
1/2 Cup crushed pineapple
4 maraschino cherries and 1 tbsp. cherry juice
1/4 Cup milk
4 ice cubes
Blend together until ice is crushed.

Orange Milkshake

by Oscar (Australia)
1/2 Cup milk
1/2 Cup orange juice
5 tablespoons ice cream
Mix all in a blender.

Peanut Butter Smoothies

Peanut Butter and Chocolate Smoothie

by Patricia (Canada)
1 Cup milk
1 tbsp. peanut butter
1 tsp. chocolate syrup
1/4 very ripe banana *
2 or 3 ice cubes, depending on desired thickness
1 tsp. vanilla extract
* You can slice up very ripe bananas and put them in a baggie or container beforehand and store in the freezer, taking a slice out each time you want to make this recipe or others containing bananas. It actually makes the smoothie thicker and colder and the very ripe bananas add a healthy dose of sweetness!

Elvis Smoothie

by Connor (MN)
1 frozen banana
1/4 Cup peanut butter
1/2 Cup vanilla yogurt
1/2 Cup milk
1 tsp honey
1/2 Cup crushed ice
Add all ingredients to blender. Blend until smooth.

Peanut Butter Banana

by Michele (Canada)
2 spoons of peanut butter
2 cups of milk
2 bananas peeled and chopped
1 spoon of chocolate syrup
2 1/2 cups of crushed ice
Mix all together in blender. Blend until smooth.

Chocolate Drizzle

by Keira (Canada)
1 sliced banana
1/4 Cup peanut butter
15 ice cubes
1 Cup milk
Blend until smooth and drizzle chocolate syrup on top of smoothie.

Peanut Butter Banana Smoothie

by Miyuki (El Paso TX)
1 banana, cut in two
spoonful of Peanut Butter
1 Cup Milk
1/2 Cup Ice
Mix ingredients together in a blender and blend until smooth.

Basic Green Smoothie

You can mix and match your green smoothies how you like. Here are the basic ingredients to start your smoothie with.

Liquid- Always include some liquid in your smoothie as this will help blend your smoothie together. However, keep in mind you don't want to add more sugar to the smoothie so choose 100% fruit juice, 100% vegetable juice, unsweetened juices, almond milk, coconut milk, low fat milk or water.

Next, add your **greens**, the most important ingredient in your GREEN smoothie! Choose from baby spinach, (my favorite) romaine lettuce, kale, (another good one) chard, collard greens, bok choy or mixed salad greens. Experiment as to which you like the most and change it up from time to time.

Fruit- frozen or fresh is the best choice. Only use canned fruit if that is all you have available as the canned also has more sugar added to the liquid. Frozen fruit works great in smoothies because it helps thicken it and you can buy a wide variety of frozen fruit.
Blueberries, bananas, apples, pineapple, berry mix, pears, peaches, grapes, you name it, most any fruit works well in a smoothie!

Extra vegetables- You may want to add more vegetables in your smoothie, although you don't have to. I like to boost the number to 5 fruits and vegetables so here are some great additions:
carrots, chopped
carrot, broccoli slaw
shredded beets
zucchini, chopped

pumpkin or cooked squash
cucumber

Experiment as to what you like, at our house my kids and I like blander flavors that don't overpower the smoothie.

From there you can add more if you choose to, such as a scoop of whey protein, flaxseed, or yogurt.

Blend together until smooth and enjoy!

Spinach Smoothies

Spinach Yogurt Smoothie

Ingredients
1/2 Cup pineapple juice
2 Cups baby spinach leaves
1 carrot, peeled and sliced
1 zucchini, peeled and sliced
1 Cup raspberries
1 banana, broken in pieces
1/2 Cup Greek or raspberry yogurt

Directions
Add all ingredients to blender and blend until smooth.

Spinach Mango

Ingredients
1/2 Cup water or 100% juice
1 Cup mango chunks
1 banana, cut in pieces
2 Cups baby spinach leaves
1 zucchini, cut in slices

Directions
Add all ingredients to blender and blend until smooth.
~To get your daily 5 in the smoothie, add one more vegetable!

Apple Blueberry Spinach

Ingredients
1/2 Cup apple juice
1/2 Cup blueberries
1 T. flaxseed
1 apple, cut in pieces
2 Cups baby spinach

Directions
Add all ingredients to blender and blend until smooth.
~To get your daily 5 in the smoothie add one more vegetable!

Blackberry Spinach Smoothie

Ingredients
1 Cup blackberries
1/2 Cup blueberries
1/2 Cup Greek yogurt
1 Cup baby spinach
1 zucchini, cut in pieces

Directions
Add all ingredients to blender and blend until smooth.
~To get your daily 5 in the smoothie add one more vegetable!

Tropical Spinach

Ingredients
1/2 Cup unsweetened pineapple juice
1 Cup pineapple chunks
1 orange, peeled and sectioned
1 Cup baby spinach leaves
1 carrot, peeled and chopped

Directions
Add all ingredients to blender and blend until smooth.

Coconut Spinach

Ingredients
1/2 Cup coconut milk
1/4 Cup chopped coconut, not sweetened
1 Cup baby spinach leaves
5-6 kale leaves, stems removed
1 banana, cut in pieces
1 T. vanilla protein powder, optional

Directions
Add all ingredients to blender and blend until smooth.

Basic Strawberry Spinach

Ingredients
1 Cup strawberry yogurt or almond milk
1/4 Cup water
1 Cup strawberries
2 Cups baby spinach leaves

Directions
Add all ingredients to blender and blend until smooth. If too thick add a little more water and blend again.
~If desired add one more vegetable such as 1/2 Cup shredded beets.

Mixed Fruits Spinach Smoothie

Ingredients
1 Cup almond or coconut milk
1 Cup frozen mixed fruits
2 Cups baby spinach leaves
1 T. flaxseed
1 Carrot, peeled and sliced

Directions
Add all ingredients to blender and blend until smooth.

Banana Strawberry Spinach

Ingredients
1/2 Cup 100% apple or other fruit juice
1 banana, cut in pieces
1 Cup strawberries
2 Cups spinach
1 zucchini cut in pieces

Directions
Add all ingredients to blender and blend until smooth.

Spinach Chocolate Berry

Ingredients
1 Cup water
2 Cups baby spinach
1 Cup mixed raspberries
1 Cup strawberries
1 T. unsweetened cocoa
1 banana, cut in pieces

Directions
Add all ingredients to blender and blend until smooth.
~To get your daily 5 in the smoothie, add one more vegetable!

Spinach Blueberry Tropics

Ingredients
1/2 Cup unsweetened pineapple juice
1 Cup blueberries
2 Cups spinach
1 orange, peeled and sectioned
1 cup broccoli coleslaw, if not available at your store use 4-5 broccoli florets

Directions
Add all ingredients to blender and blend until smooth.

Spinach Strawberry Mango

Ingredients
1/2 Cup unsweetened pineapple juice
2 Cups baby spinach
4-5 kale leaves, stems removed
1/2 Cup strawberries
1/2 Cup mango chunks
1 T. flaxseed
1/2 Cup strawberry yogurt

Directions
Add all ingredients to blender and blend until smooth.

Orange Spinach

Ingredients
1 Cup milk
1 orange, peeled and sectioned
1 banana, cut in pieces
1/4 Cup orange or vanilla yogurt
2 Cups baby spinach leaves
1 carrot, peeled and sliced

Directions
Add all ingredients to blender and blend until smooth.
~To get your daily 5 in the smoothie, add one more vegetable!

Mixed Fruit Spinach

Ingredients
1/2 Cup Greek yogurt
1 banana, cut in pieces
1 orange, peeled and sectioned
1/ Cup strawberries
2 Cups baby spinach leaves
1 cucumber, cut in slices
5-6 ice cubes

Directions
Add all ingredients to blender and blend until smooth.

It's all Green

Ingredients
1/4 Cup water
1 Cup green grapes
2 kiwis, peeled and cut in half
2 Cups baby spinach
5 broccoli florets
1 green apple, sliced

Directions
Add all ingredients to blender and blend until smooth.

Kale Smoothies

Pineapple Coconut Kale

Ingredients
1/2 Cup coconut milk
4-5 large kale leaves, stems removed
2 Cups pineapple chunks
1 cucumber, peeled and sliced
1 banana, cut in slices

Directions
Add all ingredients to blender and blend until smooth.

Tropical Kale

Ingredients
1/2 Cup unsweetened pineapple juice or orange juice
2 Cups kale leaves
1 zucchini, cut in slices
1 banana, cut in slices
1/2 Cup mango chunks
1/2 Cup pineapple chunks
1 T. flaxseed

Directions
Add all ingredients to blender and blend until smooth.

Apple Berry Kale

Ingredients
1 Cup apple juice
1 apple, sliced
1 Cup blueberries or mixed berries
1 banana, cut in slices
1/2 Cup berry yogurt
4-5 kale leaves, stems removed
1 Cup baby spinach

Directions
Add all ingredients to blender and blend until smooth.

Lemon Pear Kale

Ingredients
1 Cup pineapple chunks
1 lemon, juiced
1 Cup kale leaves
cucumber, peeled and sliced
1 pear, sliced

Directions
Add all ingredients to blender and blend until smooth.

Beet Kale

Ingredients
1/2 Cup unsweetened juice or water
1 Cup shredded beets or 1 cooked beet sliced
1 carrot, peeled and sliced
4-5 kale leaves, stems removed
1 apple, sliced
1 banana, sliced

Directions
Add all ingredients to blender and blend until smooth.

Lemon and Lime Kale

Ingredients
1 lemon, juiced
1 lime, juiced
2 bananas cut in slices
1 orange, peeled and sectioned
2 Cups kale leaves
1 zucchini, cut in slices

Directions
Add all ingredients to blender and blend until smooth.

Celery Apple Kale

Ingredients
1 Cup 100% apple juice or unsweetened pineapple juice
2 stalks celery, cut in pieces
4-5 kale leaves, stems removed
2 Cups spinach leaves
2 apples, cut in slices

Directions
Add all ingredients to blender and blend until smooth.

Mango Avocado Kale

Ingredients
1 Cup coconut or almond milk
1 mango, cut in slices or 1-2 Cups frozen mango chunks
2 Cups kale leaves
1 banana, cut in pieces
1/2 avocado

Directions
Add all ingredients to blender and blend until smooth.
~To get your daily 5 in the smoothie, add one more vegetable!

Bananas & Kale

Ingredients
1/2 Cup unsweetened pineapple juice or apple juice
2 bananas, cut in slices
4-5 kale leaves, stems removed
1/2 Cup Greek yogurt
1 zucchini, cut in slices

Directions
Add all ingredients to blender and blend until smooth.

Strawberry Kale

Ingredients
2 Cups strawberries
1 Cup apple juice
4-5 kale leaves, stems removed
1 carrot, sliced

Directions
Add all ingredients to blender and blend until smooth.
~To get your daily 5 in the smoothie, add one more vegetable!

Peach Kale

Ingredients
1/2 Cup almond milk or low-fat milk
1 peach, cut in slices or 1-2 Cups frozen peach slices
1 T. flaxseed
4-5 kale leaves, stems removed
1 celery stalk, cut in slices
1 Cup mango chunks

Directions
Add all ingredients to blender and blend until smooth.

Blackberry Kale

Ingredients
1 Cup milk, water, or juice
4-5 kale leaves, stems removed
1 1/2 Cup blackberries
1 Cup spinach leaves
1/2 Cup berry yogurt, low fat
1 T. vanilla protein powder
1 banana, cut in pieces

Directions
Add all ingredients to blender and blend until smooth.

Mixed Fruits Kale

Ingredients
1 Cup water
4-5 kale leaves, stems removed
2 Cups mixed fruits, frozen
1 Cup blueberries
1 zucchini, cut in slices
1/2 Cup broccoli coleslaw

Directions
Add all ingredients to blender and blend until smooth.

Papaya Kale

Ingredients
1 Cup pineapple juice, unsweetened
4-5 kale leaves, stems removed
1 papaya, cut in chunks
1 mango, cut in chunks or 1 Cup frozen mango chunks
1 Cup raspberries, frozen
1 carrot, peeled and sliced

Directions
Add all ingredients to blender and blend until smooth.

Watermelon Kale

Ingredients
4-5 kale leaves, stems removed
1 Cup lettuce leaves
2 Cups watermelon balls
5-6 ice cubes
1/2 Cup Greek yogurt
1 Cup strawberries

Directions
Add all ingredients to blender and blend until smooth.

Lettuce Smoothies

Good lettuces to try are Boston leaf, mixed salad greens or Romaine lettuce.

Apple Lettuce Greens

Ingredients
1/2 Cup 100% apple juice or water
1 Cup lettuce
1/2 Cup broccoli slaw, or if not available 1/2 Cup broccoli florets
1 apple, cut in slices
1 orange, peeled and sectioned
5-6 ice cubes

Directions
Add all ingredients to blender and blend until smooth.

Lettuce Pineapple Coconut

Ingredients
1/2 Cup water
1/2 Cup coconut milk
1 Cup Romaine or Boston lettuce
2 Cups pineapple chunks
1 zucchini, cut in pieces

Directions
Add all ingredients to blender and blend until smooth.

Berry Lettuce

Ingredients
1 Cup almond or low-fat milk
1 Cup lettuce leaves
1 Cup strawberries
1 banana, cut in slices
1 apple, sliced
1/2 Cup shredded beets

Directions
Add all ingredients to blender and blend until smooth.

Orange Greens

Ingredients
1 Cup orange juice
2 Cups lettuce leaves
1 Cup mango chunks or one fresh mango sliced
1 orange, peeled and sectioned
1 T. orange zest
2 carrots, peeled and sliced

Directions
Add all ingredients to blender and blend until smooth.

Lettuce & Yogurt Smoothie

Ingredients
5-6 ice cubes
2 Cups lettuce leaves
1 Cup kale leaves
1 orange, peeled and sectioned
1 banana, sliced
1 Cup strawberries
1 Cup strawberry yogurt

Directions
Add all ingredients to blender and blend until smooth.

Peach Lettuce

Ingredients
2 Cups peach slices
2 Cups lettuce leaves
1 cucumber, sliced
1 banana, sliced

Directions
Add all ingredients to blender and blend until smooth.
~To get your daily 5 in the smoothie, add one more vegetable!

Banana Lettuce

Ingredients
1 Cup apple juice or other 100% fruit juice
2 bananas, cut in pieces
2 Cups lettuce leaves
1/2 Cup broccoli slaw
1 T. flaxseed
4-5 ice cubes

Directions
Add all ingredients to blender and blend until smooth.

Fruity Lettuce

Ingredients
1/2 Cup almond milk
1 banana, cut in pieces
2 Cups mixed salad greens
1 apple, cut in slices
1 mango cut in chunks or 1 Cup frozen mango chunks
1/2 Cup mixed berries
1 carrot, peeled and cut in slices

Directions
Add all ingredients to blender and blend until smooth.

Avocado Lettuce

Ingredients
1 Cup almond milk
2 Cups mixed salad greens
1/2 avocado
1 zucchini, peeled and sliced
1 banana, sliced

Directions
Add all ingredients to blender and blend until smooth.

Super Greens

Ingredients
1 Cup vegetable juice, such as V8 juice
2 Cups mixed salad greens
4 kale leaves, stems removed
1/2 avocado
1 zucchini, peeled and sliced
1 banana, sliced
1 Cup strawberries or mixed berries
1 apple, sliced
1 T. flaxseed

Directions
Add all ingredients to blender and blend until smooth.

Mixed Green Smoothies

Zucchini Mix

Ingredients
1 Cup almond milk
1 zucchini, chopped
1 Cup baby spinach
1 Cup kale leaves
1 banana, cut in pieces
1 apple, cut in slices

Directions
Add all ingredients to blender and blend until smooth

Broccoli Greens

Ingredients
1/2 Cup low fat milk or almond milk
1 Cup baby spinach leaves
1 banana, sliced
1/2 Cup blueberries
1 Cup broccoli florets
1/2 zucchini, sliced

Directions
Add all ingredients to blender and blend until smooth.

Coconut Greens

Ingredients
1 Cup coconut milk
1 Cup baby spinach leaves
1/2 Cup shredded coconut, unsweetened
1 banana, sliced
1/2 Cup pineapple chunks
1 Cup broccoli slaw

Directions
Add all ingredients to blender and blend until smooth.

Avocado Peach Greens

Ingredients
1 Cup spinach leaves
1/2 avocado
1 banana, sliced
1 peach sliced or 2 Cups frozen peach slices
1/2 zucchini, sliced

Directions
Add all ingredients to blender and blend until smooth.

Super Greens

Ingredients
1 stalk celery, sliced
1 Cup spinach leaves
1 Cup kale leaves
1/2 cucumber, sliced
1/2 zucchini, sliced
1 green apple, sliced
1 banana, sliced

Directions
Add all ingredients to blender and blend until smooth.

Bok Choy Greens

Ingredients
2 Cups water
1 Cup bok choy leaves
1 Cup mixed berries
1 Cup kale leaves
1 banana, sliced

Directions
Add all ingredients to blender and blend until smooth.

Blueberry Greens

Ingredients
2 Cups cranberry juice
1 Cup Romaine lettuce leaves
1 Cup blueberries
1 Cup spinach
1 banana, sliced

Directions
Add all ingredients to blender and blend until smooth.

Power House Green Smoothie

Ingredients
1 Cup spinach leaves
2 stalks bok choy
1 apple, sliced
1/2 Cup blueberries
1 Cup beet sliced or shredded

Directions
Add all ingredients to blender and blend until smooth.

Kiwi Green Smoothie

Ingredients
1/2 Cup low fat milk, almond milk, or water
1 Cup spinach leaves
2 kiwis, sliced
1/2 Cup avocado
1 banana, cut in slices
1 Cup broccoli florets

Directions
Add all ingredients to blender and blend until smooth.

Chocolate Berry Greens

Ingredients
1/2 Cup almond milk or low-fat milk
1/2 Cup cherry juice
1/2 Cup baby spinach
1 T. unsweetened cocoa powder
2 Cups mixed berries
1 banana, cut in pieces

Directions
Add all ingredients to blender and blend until smooth.

Strawberry Banana Greens

Ingredients
1 Cup 100% fruit juice
1 Cup Romaine lettuce leaves
1 banana, sliced
1 Cup baby spinach leaves
2 Cups strawberries
1/2 Cup berry yogurt

Directions
Add all ingredients to blender and blend until smooth.

Green Smoothie

by Mrs. Monasterski's Class (MI)
In a blender add:
9 grapes
2 large pieces of honey dew, chopped
1 green apple, chopped
8 slices of frozen peaches
1 Cup spinach
4 crowns of broccoli
1 Cup milk
1 serving of vanilla protein powder
Add all ingredients in the blender and put blender on chop speed. When chopped you can change it to puree or blend speed until smooth. Add ice if you want. Put into a tall glass and enjoy your healthy green drink!

Printed in Great Britain
by Amazon

13849565R00079